Effectively Teaching Adult Bible Class

A Quick Read That Will Dramatically Improve Your Teaching Abilities During Your Very Next Class

By
Charles Willis

© **Guardian of Truth Foundation 2008.** All rights reserved. No part of this book may be reproduced in any form without written permission from the publisher. Printed in the United States of America. Scripture taken from the *New American Standard Bible*, Copyright 1960, 1962, 1963, 1971, 1972, 1973, 1975, 1995 by The Lockman Foundation. Used by permission. www.Lockman.org

ISBN 10: 1-58427-234-1

ISBN 13: 978-158427-234-2

Guardian of Truth Foundation
P.O. Box 9670
Bowling Green, Kentucky 42101
1-800-428-0121
www.truthbooks.net

Table Of Contents

Appreciation and Dedication 5
Foreword 7
Chapter 1: Creating An Environment Of Discussion 11
    The Purpose Of Discussion 12
    Getting The Discussion Started 14
    The Great Wait 17
    The Student's Comfort Zone 18
    Keeping The Discussion Going 20
Chapter 2: Fielding Unexpected Questions 27
    Know Your Students 27
    Prepare All You Can. 28
    Deferring Questions. 30
    Passages Or Opinion 30
Chapter 3: Benefits Of Introductory Reviewing 33
    Recall. 33
    Participation 34
    Contextual Setting. 35
Chapter 4: Preparing And Using Notes 36
    Preparing Notes. 36
    Source Materials. 37
    Making Applications 38
    Last Minute Refresher 40
    Recall or Reading? 41
Chapter 5: Raising Your Expectations. 43
    Typical Expectations 43
    Students Rise To Your Expectations 44
    Conveying Expectations. 44
    Changing Expectations 45
Chapter 6: Developing The Habits Of A Teacher 47

Enthusiasm For The topic 47
　　　Keeping A Pleasant Demeanor. 48
　　　Body Language Speaks Volumes. 49
　　　Overcoming Physical Distractions 52
　Chapter 7: Planning An Adult Curriculum 54
　　　Master Schedule. 54
　　　Weekly Schedule 56
　　　Balanced Topic Selection 57
　Chapter 8: Creating Original Materials 58
　　　Purpose Of A Workbook 58
　　　Deciding On A Topic. 59
　　　One Page Overview 61
　　　Creating A Layout 62
　　　Creating A Cover. 64
　　　Creating Content With Substance 65
　　　Creating Effective Questions 66
　　　Editing. 69
　　　Binding 70
　　　Using Purchased Workbooks 70
　Chapter 9: Practical Tips 73
　References 76

Appreciation And Dedication

This book would not have ever been brought to a state of completion without the aid in proofreading and suggestions from

Steven Estes and Ron Turnbow

Many thanks for your help.

No one has been of more help and encouragement than my wife,

Dee

Her constant belief that I have something of value to share with others continues to urge me on in my writing efforts.

For this reason I happily dedicate this book to her.

Foreword

Allow me a few moments to discuss why I have chosen to write this book. I believe it is an important consideration. At the time of this writing I have been a Christian for thirty years. I must admit to sitting through a lot of ineffective Bible classes.

The reason is simple. The people asked to teach a Bible class frequently have no experience, little experience, and/or no training or education in how to teach. There are many men in the Lord's church who have great Bible knowledge, but have no clue how to pass that knowledge on to someone else in an effective way. In every congregation there is always a need to ask a man to teach in the Junior High and High School classes. Even more so to teach an adult class. In a large congregation there may be two or three willing to teach an adult class. In smaller congregations it is typically assumed that the preacher will always teach the classes. While it is appropriate for a preacher to teach in a class environment, it is also necessary that others teach.

Teaching is a natural step in Christian growth. Hebrews 5:12 indicates there is a time when we ought to be teachers. The mature in faith are frequently shown to be teachers in Scripture (2 Tim. 2:24-26; 1 Tim. 3:2; Tit. 1:9; Acts 8:4-5). As knowledge and experience grow, it is natural to want to share this information with others, especially as the need is seen. There is a great need in our times for mature Christians who can teach. In many congregations basic Bible knowledge is lacking and many times it is weak or missing. Many believers are not grounded on basic Bible fundamentals and therefore are easily led into error and misconceptions. Mature teachers are sorely needed who can effectively teach.

Because of a lack of men who are willing to teach, some men agree to teach who feel as if their arm has been twisted. Some elder or preacher has convinced them to teach some subject, biblical letter, or workbook. Sadly, once they have agreed, there is little or no help offered. "Great, thanks for agreeing—you're on your own!" Very few individuals have a natural ability to teach. Few have studied and learned how to teach. Some have become good teachers through trial and error. Is it any wonder why so many Bible classes within the Lord's church are not very effective?

Two Styles Of Teaching

There are basically two styles of teaching which we are familiar with: lecture and discussion. My focus in this book is on discussion in a period of time which we typically call a "class." There are times when a lecture style is appropriate. Both have an appropriate place in teaching and both can be very effective. It is my opinion that effective lecturing is much more difficult than moderating a discussion. I therefore recommend that Bible Class teachers adopt the style of a discussion leader rather than a lecturer.

As you read the following chapters you may be inclined to think I am opposed to any lecture format. This is simply false, for God has said that preaching is the means by which the gospel is to be taught (1 Cor. 1:21). The gospel is "the power of God unto salvation" (Rom. 1:16). This "gospel" is also called "the word of the cross" which is the "power of God" (1 Cor. 1:18). Men will not "hear without a preacher" (Rom. 10:14). God intends for the lecture (preaching) to be the means of spreading the truth to the world. It would be foolish and sinful for me to imply or teach that lecture is implicitly wrong. Obviously it can be very effective, for the gospel spread to the entire world within the lifetime of the apostles (Acts 17:6; Col. 1:6).

There are wonderful biblical examples of sermons (lectures) which effectively bore fruit for God, both from Jesus and the apostles. Some of these are found in Matthew (5-7; 10:24-42; 23:1-39; 25:31-46), John 15:1-16:15, and Acts (2; 4:11-26; 7; 10:34-43; 13:16-41; 17:22-31). Unquestionably, lecture is effective when done well.

Jesus also demonstrates in Scripture more of what I am calling a "discussion" format where He responds to feedback and questions from others. A few examples of this can be found in Matthew 13:1-30 and John (4:7-42; 6:41-58; 7:14-31; 8:12-30, 31-59). This is merely a sampling of Jesus' teachings. While I am not trying to equate these passages to what we think of as a "Bible Class," I am trying to demonstrate that Jesus utilized different teaching styles.

My thoughts in this book are limited to the "Bible Class" environment. In such a collective study most people feel it is appropriate and acceptable to make comments, an attitude which appropriately does not exist while listening to a sermon. My intentions are to consider how to utilize effectively this time we have together as a collective, in keeping each person actively engaged and focused on the study. To apply my statements to a sermon would be a wrong and an unintended application.

In general, teachers need to learn how to moderate a discussion, how to ask effective questions, and how to lead students to a proper understanding through their personal discovery of Bible information. Effective teaching is an art. It takes courage, discipline, and desire, yet the results of your efforts will be manifest in the student's growth and interest.

It is hoped that this book will be of help to the first time teacher as well as someone who has a good bit of experience. I do believe that people can learn in a poorly taught class (I did that a lot in order to graduate from college), but that requires a lot of effort from the student. At times I fear it is more effort than the average Christian is willing or able to expend. For this reason some of our adult Bible classes are poorly attended and are not very effective.

Why me? Why am I writing this book? That's a good question. I suppose it is because I feel qualified and see there is a great need. I have a Bachelor's degree in music education from Sam Houston State University (in Huntsville, Texas) and taught Junior High School band for ten years. After receiving many awards and winning contests, I gave up the struggle in my heart and determined that I must go preach full-time. I have been preaching full-time for ten years now and have no regrets. I have been constantly honing my teaching abilities both in the private and public setting. I am a Christian, and I am an educator.

I do not have all the answers, nor am I finished learning how to teach. It is a life-long endeavor in which a person must constantly grow. Teaching is an art. It is effectively done by many different people, and accomplished in many different ways. Each person must learn what works best for himself. To be a teacher you cannot be afraid to try something you have never done before. You try it and if it works you keep doing it. If it is ineffective for you, try something else.

Throughout this book I have included quotations from professional education sources. A few are from Bible teaching sources. These all point to the truths I am trying to emphasize in this work. This has been done in an effort to demonstrate these things are not simply my good idea, but that they are accepted educational principles.

I have found these concepts and techniques effective and believe them to be effective for most teachers; therefore, I believe this material will benefit anyone who is teaching an adult Bible class.

It is with great humility and a sincere desire to help others in their teaching efforts that this book is written. That you are reading this is greatly appreciated. May we all become very effective in teaching and proclaiming the word of God.

There is nothing more rewarding

than seeing comprehension dawning

in the eyes of a student.

Charles Willis

Chapter 1
Creating An Environment Of Discussion

In most cases, the worst type of class to sit through is one that is strictly lecture taught in a dry, monotone with no attempts at making any applications. While in college I had to endure many such lessons on a variety of subjects. The other students and I had a lot of trouble staying awake! The lessons in college that were memorable were the "hands on" classes (like science labs or English classes where we were writing). Active participation is a much better learning style, yet we must admit that Bible classes at times put folks to sleep because of a lack of participation. "If your participants spend most of their time just sitting and listening, they won't learn much" (*How To Teach Adults,* 12).

Leo Myer says, "The advantage of discussion is that it can get the class totally involved in active learning" (*Teach!,* 48). A lecture format is a passive learning environment, which is why some are able to sleep. There is nothing required of a student in a lecture environment. If learning takes place it is because the student has given great attention and has learned the material with no verbalization or feedback to the teacher. "Your challenge is to reduce the amount of lecture time and to devise ways to make them active—not just passive—learners" (*Teach!,* 33). "Make students active participants in learning. Students learn by doing, making, writing, designing, creating, solving. Passivity dampens students' motivation and curiosity. Pose questions. Don't tell students something when you can ask them" (*Tools For Teaching*, 194). This is the role and purpose of the teacher, to make students active participants. This is the only way the teacher will know assuredly the lesson is being learned. While true for any subject, these truths must be emphasized for one teaching eternal truths!

Most adult Bible classes take place in the auditorium of the building. Because of this, many believe a beneficial discussion is unlikely due to the number of people in the class, or the physical make-up of the room; therefore, many never try to create an environment of discussion. *McKeachie's Teaching Tips* is a standard for adult teaching techniques. He says, "discussion methods are among the most valuable tools in the teacher's repertoire. Often teachers in large classes feel that they must lecture because discussion is impossible. In fact, discussion techniques can be used in classes of all sizes" (*McKeachie's Teaching Tips*, 35). Those who have studied educational principles, and have great experience in teaching others will quickly agree with this understanding; however, many who teach in adult Bible classes have little experience and have seldom heard of any educational principles. There is a great need for those who teach the Bible to understand more about the process of learning and the art of teaching.

The Purpose Of Discussion

Class discussion is not simply a technique of keeping people awake; rather, it is a means of edification. We may think everyone believes as we do because we are all members of the same congregation, but when we can hear a brother or sister speak passionately on a Bible topic, it encourages us and makes us appreciate each other even more. Many who will not and should not speak from the pulpit will prove themselves to be good Bible students through a discussion format. Please understand this is not merely discussion just to hear ourselves talk, but productive discussion regarding application of Scripture. My friend Henry Hudson was quick to add to any Bible discussion, and his comments were always an addition! He rarely spoke of opinion, but was always quick to provide a passage. Through this means he came to be loved and respected by all of the congregation, though he did little public speaking or teaching of classes. Had he not participated in the discussion, few would have gained from his insights or been encouraged.

A second great reason to foster discussion in a class environment is to let people know we are teaching each other. None of us knows all the answers, but together we can help each other in our understanding. "Iron sharpens iron, so one man sharpens another" (Prov. 27:17). As a teacher I have been corrected during class—and rightly so—to the extent I admitted my error and thanked the person. I've also corrected others and disagreed with some. "Expressing one's understanding or ideas and getting reactions from other students and the teacher makes a big difference in learning, retention, and use of knowledge" (*McKeachie's Teaching Tips*, 53).

A third reason, and perhaps the best reason for utilizing a discussion format is simply this: it is the only way you as the teacher will know if the students understand the concepts being taught. To be an effective teacher you must have feedback from the student. I come from a background of being a Junior High School Band Director. I had *constant* feedback about the principles I was teaching every time the students played their instruments. It is totally foreign to my knowledge of education to teach with no means of verification of understanding. It is a pointless endeavor if the teacher does not know if the student comprehends. "When you ask questions in class as you teach, you are doing informal testing" (*Teach!*, 98). It is a means of checking for understanding of the principles being discussed and taught. While this is a true and important aspect of teaching, it must be understood: "Questions that just check your participants' understanding won't encourage participation" (*How To Teach Adults*, 71).

When, for example, you are studying Galatians 3:24-25, it is important to verify student comprehension. The passage reads, "Therefore the Law has become our tutor to lead us to Christ, that we may be justified by faith. But now that faith has come, we are no longer under a tutor." Can the student tell you what Law is being discussed? What is the Tutor which we are no longer under? What is "faith" that now has come? The answers to these types of questions will tell the teacher very quickly where more teaching is needed. It may be that the class needs to discuss this passage longer than the teacher thought.

"Discussion methods are superior to lectures in student retention of information after the end of a course; in transfer of knowledge to new situations; in development of problem solving, thinking, or attitude change; and in motivation for further learning" (*McKeachie's Teaching Tips*, 58). The whole purpose of teaching is to be certain the student learns. The individual student must be considered in a class setting, which is a daunting task when there are 100 in the adult Bible class! "If we elaborate our learning by thinking about its relationship to other things we know or by talking about it—explaining, summarizing, or questioning—we are more likely to remember it when we need to use it later" (*McKeachie's Teaching Tips*, 36). A discussion environment, while more work for the teacher, is much better for the individual Bible student.

Getting The Discussion Started

This is perhaps the hardest task for the teacher, especially in a situation where students are unaccustomed to discussing. Breaking a habit of lecture presentation will be hard for the teacher and the student, yet the lasting benefits make the effort worthwhile.

Barbara Davis writes, "have in mind three or four ways to begin the discussion. . . ; if your first approach fails, try the next" (*Tools For Teaching*, 63). This technique is especially helpful when a person tries to start a discussion for the first or second time. When people fall back into the pattern of silence when we are trying to draw them into a discussion, we may have to solicit a response from them through many avenues. The easiest may be simply to tell the class you desire to have a discussion and value their thoughts and insight into the meaning of Scripture.

"You cannot get a discussion going if you ask questions that only require a one-syllable or short-phrase response" (*Tools For Teaching*, 85). Most classes are based on questions and answers about Scriptures or scriptural concepts. There is an art to asking questions in a thought provoking way. Most Bible class teachers I have studied with were not "educators" (in the professional sense) and so frequently asked questions like this (from 1 John 4):

Question: How does John describe God?

Answer: Love

This is good information to know, but there is no discussion generated. A better worded question would solicit many responses rather than the one word answer. For example:

Question: What does John mean when he says God is love?

Question: Explain the difference between having love and being love: God *is* love.

Question: How has God demonstrated He is love or must we take John's word for it?

A number of different areas can be explored if teachers will take a little more time to think through the questions they desire to ask. Care must be taken to not push the student outside his comfort zone when answering, but questions still need to be asked.

"Avoid yes/no questions. Ask 'why' or 'how' questions to lead students to try to figure out things for themselves" (*Tools For Teaching*, 85). Doug Malouf said it this way, "It should be clear that closed questions won't do much toward encouraging participation. If you want real participation, ask open questions" (*How To Teach Adults*, 69). Human nature is such that we tend to really learn things we have had to discover for ourselves. For example, parents teach us as children not to touch the hot surface but frequently until we are burned we really have not learned the lesson.

One of the best professors I had in college was Dr. Newton Strandburg who taught music theory. His method was a process of discovery, which at times was frustrating, but extremely memorable. He would give us a harmonization assignment in class which was sort of like a puzzle, with only one or two possible answers that were correct.

When we completed the assignment in class we had to bring it to him, he would play it on the piano and say "good," or "something's wrong." He rarely told you where your mistake was, preferring for the student to discover the mistake. He would frequently ask you a question or two that would hint at the problem. If a person could not solve the problem by the end of class, he would point out the errors and have him correct them. While this sounds cruel, and at times frustrating, it was also an extremely memorable and effective way to teach harmonization rules.

Those teaching Bible topics will not be able simply to tell students to go discover their mistakes. More direction and attention is necessary from the teacher. Teachers should "ask questions that require students to demonstrate their understanding" (*Tools For Teaching*, 86). If the understanding is lacking it will lead to frustration in the individual. Hopefully the teacher will pick up on this and re-teach the principle. The individual's need to be re-taught becomes very memorable, almost as much as having discovered that diamond bit of truth buried in a text. When a student recognizes he is not grasping the concept, he is more prone to pay closer attention. When the realization comes (after a second or third teaching) it is as memorable as having discovered something for ourselves. I remember studying with a young married woman on the necessity of baptism who did not agree after examining several passages. After I re-taught the same passages she broke down crying because she understood. She was upset that something so easily understood had not been taught to her before when she attended a denominational university. She had to go through a bit of "un-teaching" in order to see the light, but she became convinced. She was baptized that night.

"Keep your questions brief and clear" (*Tools For Teaching*, 85). There is nothing more frustrating to a student than to try to understand a question that takes thirty seconds to ask. Concise wording from the teacher is very helpful in focusing the thoughts of the class. At times the teacher can write a question prior to class (either in a workbook or in personal notes) which will help in generating discussion on important biblical truths.

Creating An Environment of Discussion

I believe as Bible teachers we frequently fail to create a desire for discovery in the Word of God. Perhaps this is why so few people today truly study their Bible. They have not known the pleasure and excitement of discovery in learning God's word. If we can peek through that door during a class environment, I believe more people would desire to study on their own, and they will be much more likely regularly to attend Adult Bible Classes.

The Great Wait

"The most common discussion opener is the question, and the most common error in questioning is not allowing students time enough to think. You should not expect an immediate response to every question. If your question is intended to stimulate thinking, give the students time to think. Five seconds of silence may seem an eternity, but a pause for 5 to 30 seconds will result in better discussion" (*McKeachie's Teaching Tips*, 39).

I moved to a new congregation a few years ago and did not immediately begin teaching the adult Bible classes as they were finishing up a couple of studies begun before my arrival. I had the opportunity to "observe" and participate in the classes prior to teaching. This was an eye-opening few weeks. I realized in the Sunday and Wednesday classes, three men made comments in a class of seventy-five. There was virtually no discussion. They were accustomed to lecture. When a question *was* asked, it was what I call a "regurgitation" question which was fishing for an obvious answer. I also noted that the attendance at the class period was considerably less than the worship hour on Sunday mornings, about 40-50% less (including the children's classes). When the adults do not see a great benefit from a class study, they are unlikely to bring their children to a class.

I prepared to teach my first class on a Sunday morning and I knew I had my work cut out for me. It was a new workbook I had written on 1 and 2 Thessalonians. I handed it out a week in advance. My notes were prepared and I felt I knew the topic well. It came time to begin and I knew what I had to do. I asked the first question to the class . . . and waited. It felt like a three to four minute wait, but was probably more like five to ten seconds. It was a long wait. No one answered.

I repeated the question . . . and waited. After rewording the question a third time, one of the three men who usually spoke raised his hand and gave me a good answer. What was probably equally troubling to the class was that my question could not be answered in one word, but required at least a sentence. It was not a regurgitative question, but one intended to spark thinking and discussion.

With patience (on my part) I have taught the students how to participate in a discussion format. Within three months (teaching Sunday and Wednesday) the number of participants inched upward every assembly. After five years the group discussion is terrific and most folks do not remember or perhaps even recognize the tremendous changes that have taken place in the amount of participation generated in the typical class setting, nor the improvement in the average attendance.

As a teacher you must be prepared to wait. "After you ask a question, wait silently for an answer. Do not be afraid of silence. Be patient. Waiting is a signal that you want thoughtful participation" (*Tools For Teaching*, 86). Do not answer your own question. If that becomes your habit, the students will simply learn to "out-wait" you, then let you answer. You must wait until one of them answers—and that is one of the hardest things to learn as a teacher. This is essential in creating a discussion environment. It will be most difficult for someone who has always taught in a lecture format.

The Student's Comfort Zone

Most people are not willing to embarrass themselves in a public setting, including me. That is why we as teachers prepare copious notes. We should not be surprised that students are not quick to want to attempt to answer a question they are unsure about. "Adults are afraid that they might lose their dignity. . . . Adult educators have to shelter their course participants against the possibility of humiliation. They have to watch closely to see that no one is feeling under

Creating An Environment of Discussion

attack. They have to make sure everyone is being treated with respect, and treating everyone else with respect. The tone of the group is your responsibility" (*How To Teach Adults,* 21). It may become necessary to say something to the class in general about the tone you are attempting to set, but it is just as effective and more important to demonstrate proper attitudes in your own behavior.

No one will desire to participate in a discussion when he expects to be spoken to in a demeaning manner or bluntly silenced by a teacher who desires to appear more knowledgeable. Neither will people respond to a verbal tongue-lashing from the teacher for lack of study or preparation. Praise the ones who have prepared (if you deem this important). Positive reinforcement of the behavior you desire will be more effective. I do not ask if students have prepared because that information is obvious if they are participating. In my class it is understood they are to prepare based on the workbook and the way I verbally challenge the class with questions. If they have not prepared, or prepared much, it is likely they will feel somewhat left-out or confused. I prefer to encourage study through this means, though I will quickly add that I try to explain myself fully in class, trying to leave no one in a confused state.

"When trust is present, communication is open, self-disclosure is possible, and the discussion of issues transcends small talk and word games. When trust is absent in the instructional situation, communication tends to take place only at superficial levels and learners do not become seriously engaged in the quest for knowledge and insight" (*The Religious Education Of Adults,* 207). Most people do not feel comfortable having a class discussion when a guest teacher is presenting. The relationship of trust has not been established. I have held discussion classes when I held gospel meetings, but most teachers and students are not comfortable in this environment because trust has not been established.

My experience leads me to say that the attitude of trust in the teacher will take three to four class periods to establish, perhaps longer. During this period it is essential that the teacher be extra careful of his reactions to comments from the class. Even if a wrong answer is given, be delicate in saying it was wrong. Harsh or abrupt language discourages. People need to see and hear that you will behave as a Christian in the way you treat others in the Bible class. They will then become comfortable trusting you will treat them with love when they add to a discussion.

Every congregation will have a different comfort zone, as will the individual. If (as in my previous example) the class is accustomed to lecture, the comfort zone will be extremely narrow. It may be wider for those who are more mature and thereby confident of their answers. This means a lot of judgment needs to be exercised by the teacher to know how to word questions (especially those not on the lesson sheet).

Great care should be taken to consider how far to push the class into their discomfort zone. A dangerous question (to the student) is one that he risks answering wrong. Questions that begin with "explain," "compare and contrast," or "what application" may be considered too uncomfortable for folks to try to answer. Safe questions would begin with wording like "in your opinion," "what do you think," and "what does Scripture say." The teacher can become easily frustrated with a lack of discussion and not realize it is a result of the type of questions being asked. Simply back off or restate the question into something more comfortable. Eventually the class will come to recognize it is "safe" to answer a question outside their comfort zone.

Keeping The Discussion Going

It is great to get a discussion started, but a common problem will arise: the discussions will be short. This will be natural as a teacher attempts a discussion format for the first few times. Many teachers find it difficult to keep the discussion going.

Many well-intentioned Bible class teachers cut off discussion by jumping back in to read the notes they have so diligently prepared. This prevents discovery from taking place in the class and simply provides the teacher opportunity to share his discoveries. A good

Creating An Environment of Discussion

attitude to take is: "Avoid the temptation to respond to every student's contribution. Instead, allow students to develop their ideas and respond to one another (*Tools For Teaching*, 76). There will be opportunity for the teacher to share his points with the class, but this method allows the class to share points with one another and with the teacher. Many times the points I plan to make are brought out in such discussions. The class' discovery of the text went where I wanted to go—but I did not have to lecture! This is ideal!

A teacher who is good at leading discussion oriented classes will be a good moderator. This is as far away from a lecturer as can be imagined. "In a discussion, you should say very little. Let the class carry the discussion, with comments from one person triggering comments and opinions from others. Your role is to keep the discussion from running too far off the subject, and to ask questions to involve those who are reluctant to speak up" (*Teach!*, 48). To moderate a group of adults there must still be discipline and order in the room. A very important aspect of being the moderator is in yielding the floor to a speaker. I would advise you to ask people to raise their hands, rather than just speaking out. Maintain some control and decorum over the class. It is not frowned upon if someone feels compelled to speak out without being called on (and this will happen), rather the moderator is happy that others desire to participate. In a smaller congregation or class (of say "ten to fifteen) this will not be needed, but it is very helpful in classes with more than thirty students. In classes of fifty or more this is essential.

The teacher/moderator should not feel obligated to say something after each person's comment. "You needn't give a verbal response to every student. By nodding or pointing, you can keep the focus on your student's responses rather than shift attention to yourself" (*Tools For Teaching*, 89). It is hard to overcome the urge to speak when you are wearing a microphone, yet it is often beneficial to the class to be a listener! Much can be learned from the class if the teacher will listen to their comments, discussion, and questions with a mindset of determining if they have learned the point. That information will dictate whether a response from the teacher is necessary.

The use of non-verbal interactions will be very helpful. We convey so much with facial expressions and body language in our everyday conversations. Recognize we do the same thing in the teaching environment. "Use nonverbal clues to encourage participation. For example, smile expectantly and nod as students talk. Maintain eye contact with students. Look relaxed and interested" (*Tools For Teaching*, 78). "Use nonverbal clues to maintain the flow. For example, hold up your hand to signal stop, to prevent one student from interrupting another" (*Tools For Teaching*, 69). Point to the next person, or call out his name and let him respond to the previous person. At times I have experienced a discussion going back and forth between two or three people with me calling on each one. I was still in control but allowed the discussion. This is very helpful when one of the speakers is an elder.

Once a discussion format has been initiated, the teacher begins to get in the habit of letting everyone speak. Just because a person has his hand up does not mean that you must call upon him. For example, if there are five minutes left in the class period and you desire to finish a point—finish it. It is a good problem to have to ignore some who want to make comments. I would not make this a regular habit as it would inhibit the environment of discussion.

Another example may be of a brother who always seems to interject an off-topic comment, or has to tell a joke. I love my brethren, but sometimes I don't think they realize how disruptive some of these things can be to a good discussion climate, and how they pull the focus away from the word of God; therefore, I sometimes do not call on them. At times, who you call on will be as important in generating discussion as what he might say.

As is often the case when discussion is desired, someone will bring up a point that shifts the discussion off on a tangent. This can be a very good thing! "Participation is not an end in itself. For many purposes widespread participation may be vital; for others it may be detrimental. But you want to create a climate in which an important contribution is not lost because the person with the necessary idea did not feel free to express it" (*McKeachie's Teaching Tips*, 46). Do not be afraid as a teacher to explore some of these areas. They serve several purposes.

1. You demonstrate to the class that their discussion has an impact on the class—that it is not so stymied or rigid that it must follow your outline.

2. You demonstrate to the class that you are also learning from the discussion. Frequently the best comments from the class come from such extemporaneous spiritual discussions. Applications to a text may not have been seen by the teacher. Certainly there are others in the congregation as wise, or wiser than the teacher.

3. You demonstrate to the class that there are no dumb questions. In seeking to verify understanding in the student's minds, they may ask for a further explanation or a further application. These are terrific teaching opportunities.

Sometimes the discussion does not go where you anticipated. The teacher needs to take control of the discussion. He can choose to continue down the unplanned tangent, or he can stop that discussion and politely return to the topic we are studying. "Bring the discussion back to the key issues. If the discussion gets off track, stop and describe what is happening: 'We seem to have lost sight of the original point. Let's pick up the notion again that. . .'" (*Tools For Teaching*, 69). I find that at times re-reading a key passage under discussion, or re-focusing the class on the context does much to eliminate the discussion from straying off topic. There is nothing worse than a teacher who feels obligated to follow every tangent brought up in every class. The student feels as if no progress is being made to finish the study at hand. Frankly speaking, it frustrates the teacher also.

Invariably a wrong answer will be given, or a falsehood will be presented from a text based on faulty logic or lack of knowledge. "Tactfully correct wrong answers" (*Tools for Teaching*, 80). Students will learn more quickly to trust a teacher based on how he deals with an incorrect answer than with how he deals with a correct answer.

Do not be afraid to indicate a wrong response was given. I have heard some teachers try to work every comment into the truth being presented no matter how far off topic, and no matter how absurd, simply because they did not want to give offense to a brother or sister by telling him or her that he or she was wrong. Tact is necessary. Some helpful phrases include:

- That's not quite right.
- I think I would disagree with that.
- Is that what the passage says?
- I would partially agree with you.
- Help me understand your point when the passage says . . .

The point is to not cut off the student's desire to participate simply because he gave an answer that was wrong. In my life, most of the memorable lessons involved me giving an incorrect answer. We learn from our mistakes.

The last time this happened in one of my classes a good sister had obviously missed the point of a passage and made a comment totally off topic and frankly was wrong because it was out of context. I kindly said I disagreed and stated why by re-focusing the class back to the context. After the class she thanked me for the way I dealt with her when she obviously was wrong. Teachers need to realize how important these moments are to all the students. They are trust-building moments!

Barbara Davis suggests: "Be alert for signs that a discussion is breaking down. Indications that a discussion is not going well include the following:

- Excessive hair splitting or nit-picking
- Repetition of points
- Private conversations
- Members taking sides and refusing to compromise
- Ideas being attacked before they are completely expressed
- Apathetic participation" (*Tools For Teaching*, 71).

While all of these are not always seen in a Bible Class discussion, they are all possible signs. The first three in particular are very common signs that should alert the teacher that the discussion is breaking down.

"Present material in ways that are meaningful to students. If you can relate what you are teaching to something already meaningful, relevant, or important to students, they are more likely to understand and remember the new material" (*Tools For Teaching*, 181). Bible study and Bible discussion that makes no application is not study. One of the hardest aspects of being a moderator is to take the comment from someone else and expand on it in making a meaningful application. This is a mark of an excellent teacher because these are unplanned applications. Do not be afraid to explore applications this way in front of a class—however you may want to tell them "let me think out loud a moment" or "has anyone else had this thought" Care should be taken (as always) never to present false doctrine. If unsure, it is better not to attempt an application. You can always ask if someone else can think of an application.

One of the best ways to present meaningful material is to constantly relate the truth to your own life. Share with the class some of your frustrations as a parent, a spouse, a child, a preacher, an elder. Speak from your own experiences. Not that the teacher should spend long periods speaking of himself, but a simple acknowledgment of the problems "we have," or "I have struggled with that." Let them know you are one of them, thereby removing the barrier which sometimes exists between students and the teacher. They will appreciate your personalization of the text, and will likely see similar applications in their own lives which they may then want to share. Let them share their thoughts.

It may become necessary to ask follow-up questions, especially if "training" a congregation to have good discussions in class. You may need to lead them with a few obvious questions before asking a more difficult question by way of application or comparison with false religions. Sometimes these leading questions can be prepared in notes before hand, but often it will need to be done off the top of the head. A teacher needs to anticipate where he wants the discussion to go, and generally it will follow his plan.

"You can involve more students by asking whether they agree with what has just been said or whether someone can provide another example to support or contradict a point" (*Tools For Teaching*, 78). In this manner the teacher has not really responded to the comment, but has solicited a response from the class. This is a good way to keep the discussion going.

SUMMARY

An environment of discussion is a great blessing to everyone in the class. It provides not only opportunity to teach and encourage each other, but also the ability to discover what the text is teaching. It is healthy for a congregation to have such discussions. I would find it disturbing if saints met regularly and did not have such spiritual discussions (in or out of the assemblies). A class period is a great opportunity to aid a congregation in becoming closer, learning more about God's word, and growing closer to God as individuals.

Chapter 2
Fielding Unexpected Questions

There is nothing that strikes more fear into the heart of an inexperienced teacher than the prospect of an unexpected question. I firmly believe this is one of the main reasons many people never teach an adult Bible class. Like students, teachers also do not like to go outside their comfort zone. The fear of the unexpected question revolves around pride. No one wants to appear unable to answer a question, so logic says "why teach?" Let someone else do it. These fears are unfounded, especially within the Lord's church. My experience has been that you will never stand before a more sympathetic and understanding group of people. They will endeavor to encourage you, even if you are not doing such a great job. Occasionally there is a brother or sister who will choose to demonstrate his/her superior knowledge, and thus discourage—but this is unusual. A good response to a difficult question is to pause and smile, looking at the one who asked! You may be surprised to see everyone else just as uncomfortable as you. Admit your difficulty in answering.

There is nothing wrong with not knowing an answer. The only one who could answer any unexpected question was Jesus, because it was not unexpected! All the rest of us at times will have to say "I don't know" or "I'll find out." The fact that the question is unexpected probably means it is not on topic and no one would have prepared for it. Do not be shocked when this happens. It *will* happen.

Know Your Students

One of the greatest aids to the teacher in fielding unexpected questions is to know your students. Just a little time in a Bible class will inform the attentive teacher of who asks these type of questions. One good brother I have worshipped with often asks unusual questions and afterward will tell me he knows he is asking unexpected questions. In his mind the question applies to the discussion, but others do not see how. He may be leading the teacher into an area he wants to discuss and chooses to introduce the subject with a tough question.

A simple technique would be to avoid calling on that brother or sister. This cannot be done all the time, but some avoidance (at choice times) can be an effective technique for keeping the class on topic. I tend to call on this type of participant less frequently when handling a difficult or opinionated topic and more frequently on fundamental issues.

Nevertheless, there will still be the occasional unexpected question that will come our way. Knowing the person asking the question can perhaps give some insight into how to respond. Things to know about the person might include: how long he has been a Christian; his religious background; his marital status; his employment; relationship problems he might be having; his stand on some religious "issues" or "thoughts." Many other things quickly run through the mind about the person asking the question. It is good to consider such information, but not to the extent that you fail to hear and understand the question.

"Teaching by discussion differs from lecturing because you never know what is going to happen. At times this is anxiety-producing, at times frustrating, but more often exhilarating. It provides constant challenges and opportunities for both you and the students to learn" (*McKeachie's Teaching Tips*, 55).

Prepare All You Can

Depending on the subject matter, some questions can be anticipated. A wise teacher will study to some extent into tangent areas and perhaps make a few anticipatory notes, or record a few appropriate passages. This can be a life-saver in the desperate moments after the hard question is raised. I recommend placing a separate sheet at the back of your comments, or under your Bible so that they are quickly brought to hand. Expect the unexpected.

More importantly than being concerned about the unexpected question is the need to immerse yourself into the context of what is being studied. Even if a topical study is underway, teach the class from a select number of passages in their respective contexts. This is especially important when engaged in a book study. Everything said should revolve around a focused theme. "One of the biggest problems in teaching by discussion is focus. Getting the discussion headed in the right direction and keeping it there requires that both students and the instructor be focused on the same questions" (*McKeachie's Teaching Tips*, 41).

For example, in a study of Ephesians, a theme is presented: all spiritual blessings are in Christ Jesus (1:3). Chapter 1 then enumerates many of those blessings. Chapter 2 speaks of our relationship without being in Christ, then how the Jew and Gentile are now one in Christ. Chapter 3 describes how we came to learn about the blessings in Christ—through the inspired message. Chapters 4-6 then give our responsibilities and duties as those who are enjoying these spiritual blessings. There are other approaches which could also be beneficial to a book study, but nothing could be better than a contextual study.

The teacher's preparation is vital. "The key to good lecturing is careful preparation" (*Teach!*, 43). If true about lecturing, it must be more so about leading a discussion. Not only must there be a familiarity with the text being studied, but also how it relates with the remainder of the book. What precedes and follows the current text is vital to our understanding. I am speaking of chapters before and after. For example: it is difficult to study the Kings of Judah without knowing the attitude and reign of the current king's father and grandfather. Keeping the class discussion on topic and in context will go a long way toward reducing unexpected questions. A teacher cannot study and prepare too much.

Deferring Questions

A good technique for the novice teacher (and at times the mature) is to defer answering the question to another person in the class. It is appropriate for an elder to answer a question at any time. I have occasionally said, "brother Bob, how would you answer that?" or, "I'm going to defer to one of the elders" and waited for one of them to speak up. If no elder is present, anyone in the class could be called upon. This serves several purposes: (1) It gives a wiser person an opportunity to answer when you are not prepared. (2) It provides the teacher time to think how he would respond. (3) It tells the class you are also a student and engaged in learning.

One of the worst attitudes to adopt as a teacher is that you are the only one in the room teaching. The teacher is not alone. Defer to others. Listen to others. Give others opportunity to speak and teach. Again, this is the mindset of a teacher who is a moderator.

Some questions need to be deferred till another time. Off topic comments and questions will occur, and the teacher must decide *how* to steer the class away from the topic. The simplest course is again to point to the context. Politely state the comment is not pertinent to the present context. Be certain to indicate your willingness to discuss the topic, just not at the present time. Ask them to be sure and contact you later that day, or later in the week (leave the ball in their court). There are times I pursue the student after class, but if this is something important to them they will seek me out. My experience has been that the more I stay in the context, or on the topical subject, the fewer off-topic comments are made.

Passages Or Opinion

The best way to respond to any unexpected question is to provide a passage of Scripture. My father's advice many years ago was to let Scripture speak whenever possible and then be quiet. Folks find it hard to argue with Scripture. Even Jesus was fond of answering questions with Scripture (Matt. 4).

There are times when a passage does not come to mind. The worst thing a teacher can do is to give his opinion, after all, this is a *Bible* class. A wise teacher will seldom respond with opinion, primarily because our opinions are often not based on Scripture and we may be proven wrong.

It is appropriate for a teacher to admit "I don't know." It is a valid and appropriate answer. When fielding such a question, I will often ask the same thing of the one who questioned me. They frequently have an answer but wanted to hear me first. After they respond, the teacher may have a better idea of how to answer. Even then, "I don't know" is a good answer.

If you tell a person you will study something and get back with him, be sure to do just that! Be a man of your word. Practice what you preach. A simple phone call, or a note can take care of a follow-up discussion. These are often very insightful and uplifting types of discussions. Do not be fearful of studying with anyone. The teacher will always benefit the most from any study.

Care should be taken as to how much time will be dedicated to a tangent, or an unexpected question. Depending on the degree of discussion generated, and what time constraints you have, such discussions can be very rewarding for a congregation. Perhaps the best personal example of this occurred a few years ago. The congregation had just overcome a difficult period when one brother unsuccessfully attempted to introduce a false doctrine. Several weeks later a question was asked that skirted some of the same issues of that time. I decided to let people talk about it. The question came in the first five minutes of class, and I did not talk the rest of the class period! We had forty minutes of class discussion which I moderated. It was extremely beneficial and could not have been planned. That is an extreme example. More common is the need to shut discussion off and regain control of the flow of the discussion. I mention this to indicate a teacher must use discretion and wisdom in controlling discussion. We should all pray for wisdom as Solomon did.

Redirecting discussion must be done tactfully. It is easy to bruise egos and feelings if we are not careful. A class teacher has no scriptural right to ignore passages about how to treat a brother, particularly an elderly brother. Be respectful and courteous, but tell the class there is a need to move on and return to the subject matter. Sometimes this feels like a "cold break" because the discussion wandered so far off topic. The teacher's responsibility is to keep the class on subject. If the teacher will not do it, who will?

Fielding unexpected questions is never pleasant. Every teacher mentally groans when such a question is asked. How we respond, how we handle such questions, will to a great extent determine if other students will ask questions or participate in the discussion. Look at the unexpected question as an opportunity to create an environment of discussion in which everyone is comfortable speaking up.

Chapter 3
Benefits Of Introductory Reviewing

Most Bible classes will start with a prayer. That is appropriate and should continue. Some teachers say "amen" and launch into the text for the day. The teacher had obviously been mentally preparing himself, but he does a great disservice to the students. They also need to mentally prepare for the study.

All students (children and adults) respond well to a quick review process. This introduction period serves several purposes: recall, participation, and contextual setting. All of these benefit a group study.

Recall

During the first class on a new topic the introductory period may be more of a check of general knowledge about the topic. This period may contain more lecture than usual at the beginning of a class. The teacher should be trying to convey the background of a book, or purpose for studying the material at hand.

The teacher must give the direction for the study and hopefully a theme for the class. For example, in studying Ephesians emphasis may be on "all spiritual blessing are in Christ" (Eph. 1:3). A single verse or phrase is best for describing a book theme. For Hebrews it may be the use of the word "better," which is found in many chapters. In a topical study the teacher has much more liberty in setting this theme.

At each of the subsequent class periods the teacher should review the thematic material covered in the first introduction. Have students recall this information by asking a few simple questions: What is the theme? What have I emphasized as the key passage? What is the purpose of this study? This technique forces everyone to focus his mind on the topic and brings to the foreground recent studies on the topic.

Participation

An introductory review also sets the tone for the class. It lets the students know you want their participation and welcome it. I would encourage all teachers to smile within the first three minutes of every class. A smile can do amazing things in getting people to participate. It will render much more positive results than a stare, a pointing finger or calling upon an individual.

I frequently use the brief review period to foster participation. Try to get at least three different people to answer a question with something more than a one-word response. As the weeks go by in the same study, some of these questions will be repetitive—that is good! It gives the teacher the ability to perhaps get a response from someone who does not frequently speak up. If they have been present for weeks, everyone should know how to answer some of these questions.

At first the teacher will likely need to write down a few key questions. These could perhaps be asking about the theme of a previous chapter, or some key concept that carries throughout the study. Take care to write the question well, and use it as often as needed to emphasize the importance of the content. Some questions do not need to be asked every week, such as: who wrote the book, when was this written, or where is Ephesus. These could occasionally be effectively asked, but more questions about the content of the study would be better.

A review should be at least one minute and not longer than three. You may be surprised how many quick questions can be covered in one minute. Try not to allow the class to become bogged down in the review since there is new material to be covered. If the review drags out it becomes ineffective. Students begin to think this material was covered in previous lessons. The over-extended review tends to lead to repeated discussions from previous class periods, which is unnecessary and unproductive. It is the teacher's job to keep the review moving and to end the review at an appropriate time.

Toward the end of the study it is profitable to have students write the review into their workbook or notes. This serves as additional thematic material when they hopefully return to this material in the future. By this point they should all be able to answer the questions, but few would have thought of writing it down. The teacher will appear to be wise and thoughtful for having made the suggestion.

Contextual Setting

This last beneficial purpose of an introductory review is in my estimation the most important, especially in a study of a book of the Bible. Biblical study is not applicable without a proper understanding of the context. Great care should be taken to weave contextual comments into every class period, especially the review.

For example, in studying Galatians it is very helpful to understand the book was written because of false teachers introducing Old Testament practices into the Church. It is helpful to restate how amazed Paul was that they were deserting the truth for "a different gospel" (Gal. 1:6), that he asked "who has bewitched you" (Gal. 3:1), and the Old Law has been taken away and we are "no longer under a tutor" (Gal. 3:25). This weaving of passages into the introductory review does much to set the context for the particular verses being considered in the current class period. It also helps the student retain a very good picture of what the book is about. Since it is a very common practice at most congregations to study through several books in one year, it is highly recommended that teachers regularly take the time to review at the beginning of each class. You and your students will benefit from this effective technique.

Chapter 4

Preparing And Using Notes

Everyone who teaches an adult class understands the need to prepare. Few understand what to do with their notes once they have been written. The purpose of this chapter is to help the teacher understand how best to utilize these aids during class.

Preparing Notes

Perhaps it is simplistic, but all prepared notes need to be logically laid down and legible. Whether hand written or typed, speaking notes need to be very clear. Consider that at times you will be glancing at notes while you are speaking. Nothing worse could occur than for a teacher to lose his place in his notes, or suddenly realize his notes are illegible.

It is strongly recommended that a formal outline format be followed. Whether you are using questions handed out to the class or are progressing through a verse-by-verse study, use indentions to keep them visible, clean and clear. Use a simple font and at a size that is comfortable to you. Better to use more pages than having notes so small you cannot read them. The following example is a good format:

    I. Main Point / Question / Verse
        A. Sub-point
            1. Comment
            2. Comment
        B. Sub-point
            1. Comment

On a full page, this format is very easy to read and allows for visually quick glances to get a thought. Other formats are just as efficient. Something like this should be used regularly so that you are comfortable using your notes.

Full sentences are encouraged. Convey the entire thought, rather than just sketchy details. This is especially helpful when reviewing these notes in the future. Care should also be taken to store these in such a way that they will not be lost. A three-ring binder or folder works well in addition to digital storage.

Common sense says to prepare notes as far in advance as possible. For those who teach on a regular basis, a good habit is to prepare notes at least seven to eight days in advance. This ensures that enough material is prepared, should you need more. More importantly, it allows the teacher to have a good understanding of where the class is currently at and where the study is headed next week. Therefore, preparing in advance aids the contextual understanding. An additional benefit from preparing further in advance than twenty-four hours is that the teacher will need to re-examine his notes, which serves as a refresher. I would recommend this sometime the day before the class is to be held, in addition to immediately prior to class.

Source Materials

First and last, use your Bible. Various translations can be of some help, but do not stray far from your Bible. In other words, stay with one translation as much as possible. Frequently skipping from one translation to another will confuse students. Use a good translation that is accurate to the original languages and is easily understood.

A consideration of the Hebrew or Greek is a necessity, but base such word studies on the same translation. Original language studies can be shallow or deep and can include many resources. I have used many if not most of the common books available and find that I keep returning to *Strong's Concordance*. If I had to pick one book in addition to my Bible, it would have to be Strong's. A good reference library will be of invaluable help in most cases, but I still recommend sticking to your Bible. Use Scripture to discuss Scripture. Whenever possible, use a biblical example or story to illustrate the point of the passage being studied.

Making Applications

It is important in any study thoroughly to understand a passage in the context in which it is embedded. This understanding should be conveyed to the class as well. This is very important when engaged in a topical study that will examine passages from many places in Scripture. Work to limit yourself in a topical study to three or four main passages and the student's understanding will improve. Too often in a topical study we try to provide every passage that uses a word, phrase, or concept. Some material is studied which lists dozens of passages. This is unrealistic in that students will not typically examine this many passages in their context in preparation for a forty-five minute class. It is better to stay focused on a few passages.

Only when the passage is understood in its context should any consideration be given to the application. Some teachers never get to the application. They see the importance of teaching the concept from the passage and spend a great deal of time on this to the extent the application is seldom made. For most students the understanding is lost without the application! Therefore it is vital the teacher is conscious of the time remaining so that the applications are made.

If working from a workbook, the application questions may or may not be provided. Some workbooks have a section labeled application questions, but which are not in fact application questions. An application takes the information in a passage and relates it to our modern situation. Many times the application is obvious, being the same for us as for them. Better applications point to areas not typically considered. Creating questions is an art. This is nowhere more apparent than in dealing with applications.

To formulate an application question you are encouraged to pay close attention to every word in each verse. Build your thoughts on the use of one word or phrase. A good technique is to utilize a scenario from which the students are to respond. Revisiting the biblical concept in a modern setting forces the student to understand the teaching of Scripture. For example, when discussing 1 John 4 dealing with brotherly love, a scenario might depict a poor reaction to a brother or sister. The question might be "How would you have responded?" or perhaps, "What is a scriptural response?" Both will generate discussion about the scenario and more importantly about what the Scriptures are teaching us.

Some may be thinking that applications are difficult or impossible in some Bible passages. Books like Leviticus and Deuteronomy or passages which relate specific laws appear to be difficult to generate applications. This is when the teacher must earn the title of "teacher" and bring these passages to life. While we do not live under the Old Law, we are to learn from it. Emphasis can be made on the differences between the old and new covenants, or even how much better the new covenant is than the old covenant. Even an application dealing with the attitude of God is beneficial from such passages. A difficult passage for the teacher is even more difficult for the student! Therefore, a good teacher will work especially hard to generate thoughtful applications from a difficult text.

Applications may need to be inserted in a workbook study. If the writer has not provided enough questions, or some that are appropriate, it becomes the teacher's job to provide them. Trying for three to four good application questions will provide enough material to generate discussion.

Human nature tells us to follow the outline that has been provided for us to teach from (assuming we are using a purchased workbook). Even if we are studying from material we wrote, we still tend to follow the outline exactly. I would encourage you to consider carefully when you plan to introduce an application question. A lot of adult Bible classes I have been involved in as a student saved all the application questions till the end. Invariably we would have three to five minutes to discuss some really great applications. The class would end and the teacher would tell us to prepare the next lesson for the following week. The applications were never really emphasized. I reiterate: For most students, the understanding is lost without the applications. Thoughtful teachers will scatter applications and discussions throughout the class period.

What would the class be like if it were started with an application question? It was assumed the students had studied the material in advance (telling the students of your expectations). It would immediately require discussion and comments. It may be this is an application based on material studied in the previous lesson. This could be an advantageous form of review. This would be preferable to cutting off discussion at the end of a class.

I would encourage all teachers to insert a few good application questions into every class period. It is the easiest and most effective way to check for the student's understanding of the material being studied. Very quickly you will learn as the teacher if you need to move on or if you need to re-teach. Having these questions prepared in advance is very helpful, even if they must be written in the margins of a page.

Last Minute Refresher

Familiarity with the material being taught is essential. A worst case scenario is to write the notes the night before and then try to coherently present them the next morning. I find that things frequently get jumbled in my brain under such circumstances. My understanding improves drastically if I have notes prepared several days in advance and can read over them a few times prior to class. It is therefore recommended that you work a week or two in advance in preparing your notes.

An hour before class is to begin you are encouraged to read over your notes yet again. The last thing you should do before you stop studying is to read over the main text a time or two. This will help in keeping the sequence and context of the coming presentation clearly in mind. It is best to have no interruptions during this process. You will have to find a time that works best for you, but I would recommend it be on the same day as the study and that it be within no more than ninety minutes of the time class begins.

Recall or Reading?

I will confess to reading class notes, but not always, and not frequently. When I am presenting a delicate point, or a point with which some in the congregation have trouble, I will read my notes carefully so as to not be misunderstood. This is not a bad thing, but a good one; however this should not be the habit of the teacher. When reading we are not opening the door for discussion. We will find it hard even to see the student's faces and know if they are following what we are saying.

You are encouraged to become so familiar with your notes that you know what you plan to present. You are familiar with any stories as examples. You know what the reference says you plan to examine. The ideal scenario for the teacher is to recall the notes by just a cursory glance on occasion. You are not expected to memorize your notes.

Invariably someone in class will mention a point you plan to cover fifteen minutes later. It may not be appropriate to discuss it at that point, and the teacher has the opportunity to delay the discussion till later; but, there may be nothing wrong with discussing it right then. When you know what you want to talk about, you can allow the discussion to flow in this manner from one thought to another without seeming to stick rigidly to your notes. In fact you are still teaching from your notes, though you may be turning backward and forward during the class! No one needs to know that but you.

It is helpful to verbalize your notes prior to class, or least some of the more difficult portions. To check your own understanding, say out loud what you plan to say to the class. It may be that your presentation of the things prepared is harder than expected. This is a technique that also works well in personal work. Practice expressing yourself in private before you speak to the individual or the class. This works amazingly well! It enables the teacher to recall notes by glancing down, rather than reading.

Nothing will help the teacher more than well prepared notes. Yet, they remain an aid during the class period. Try not to be tied to your notes, or the lectern. Be a part of the class by moving around and looking at as many people as possible. Recall allows you to physically return to your notes periodically, then continue speaking. This is a much better approach when teaching adults.

Chapter 5
Raising Your Expectations

Typical Expectations

"Probably the best answer to why the adult classes are like they are is that we've spent a lifetime of training the adults to behave the way they do! While they're small children, they are involved and excited and participating because we go to great pains to see that the classes are prepared that way. We worry about not keeping them busy, about keeping their attention, about getting them to sing and move and be a vital part of the learning experience. As the students grow older, they are allowed to listen more and more and participate less and less, until finally they are adults and don't have to do anything" (*Success At Bible Teaching*, 51).

Some congregations have no expectations of the adults in the class environment. This means they have no lesson to prepare, there is no discussion, and if Bibles are opened that is considered a bonus. Sadly this occurs in some places, but thankfully not most.

More common is a poor expectation of adults. They are to return with their materials and Bibles, but they are not expected to have prepared or to discuss in class. If they are expected to prepare, the depth of study is shallow. Answers in class are typically just a quotation of a verse or a simple answer. The level of study in many congregations is immature, weak, and lukewarm. What happened to being zealous of good works?

Students Rise To Your Expectations

Think back to your days in Junior High and High School. Can you remember being with the same group of students in three or four different classes? Can you also remember how some of these same students would behave differently depending on the teacher's expectations? The good student might revert to a talkative, inattentive student for the teacher with low expectations. In contrast, the goof-off or lazy student will do an amazing amount of work for a teacher (or coach) who demands it.

"Hold high but realistic expectations for your students. Research has shown that a teacher's expectations have a powerful effect on a student's performance" (*Tools For Teaching*, 195). Too often the reason an adult Bible class does not work is because the teacher has little to no expectations from the students. When asked to teach an adult class, the new teacher often thinks he must "entertain" or lecture to the class for forty-five minutes. He feels as if everything is up to him. He is correct, but fails to realize there are other adults in the room who need, want, and should participate in the study.

It is not too much to expect adults to prepare for a study by reading their Bibles and answering a few questions. I strive to keep student preparation time to about twenty minutes per class period. It is also not too much to expect students to participate in discussion or in asking questions. If the facility allows, it is not too much to expect adults to work in smaller groups and return to the entire group with a conclusion. Students will do whatever is expected of them (generally). You will always have some with a poor attitude who will not prepare or participate.

Conveying Expectations

The need to convey expectations will only be necessary at the beginning of a study (usually). You emphasize this by asking them to prepare. When teaching, you must then assume they have prepared. Sometimes those who have not prepared may feel it is difficult to follow the discussion. They are to be encouraged to prepare more.

For some reason some adult teachers find it difficult to say things to the class regarding expectations. Some would never ask this: "please read all of 3rd John every day between now and the next class to familiarize yourself with the text" or "try to read all of Colossians in one sitting before class." This is not too much to ask and adults who are serious about Bible study will make the time if you simply ask them.

Written expectations are also very helpful. This is most useful in a workbook you have prepared. Providing spaces for answers relays to the student that you expect them to answer the questions. Giving a Bible reading for the lesson conveys a need to read. Specific instructions on each question can convey varying expectations.

If you convey an expectation, there also needs to be an explanation as to why you expect the student to do this, especially with verbal instructions. No one likes to waste his time.

Changing Expectations

Do not be afraid to ask students to do something they have never done before. Again, if you expect, they will generally do it. If you are introducing new methods, take it slow. Things outside the realm of experience will likely be considered strange, unusual, perhaps even unlawful!

State clearly to the class that you are asking them to do something different. Speak of why you want them to do this. Convey what you suspect may be some of their reservations and how you have felt about doing it. Smile a lot. Continue to tell them you want them to do this.

During the class which incorporates the changed expectation, you as the teacher must "enforce" the new expectation. In other words if your attitude about the expectation has not changed from the previous behavior, the students will not adopt the new behavior or try the new thing. For example: if the class is accustomed to answering true/false questions by stating "true" or false," they will think it strange when you expect them to provide a passage proving their answer. In class you must then ask for the passage and look at it to determine if it indeed supports their answer. Without the teacher's expectation the students will simply revert or continue to model the old behavior.

The effective Bible class teacher will work to convey expectations that are realistic but which also challenge their fellow saints to stretch and grow.

Chapter 6
Developing The Habits Of A Teacher

Enthusiasm For The Topic

Imagine for a moment that an employer calls a meeting of the employees to discuss an important matter. Everyone gathers in the meeting room, the boss thanks everyone for coming and turns the meeting over to a department supervisor. This man walks to the lectern, in no hurry, and spends more than thirty seconds messing with his paperwork. When he finally looks up at the gathered employees he gives a grimace and says: "It is my joy to announce to you that at this meeting we will be covering all laws and company rules in regard to internet use." He gives a rather deep sigh, glances once more at the employees, turns his back to them, and proceeds to read a video presentation he had prepared in advance. When it has finished twenty minutes later he asks: "Any questions?" Everyone can recognize this department supervisor had been saddled with a task he did not desire. There was no genuine concern for the subject, nor in being certain the employees understood why this was a concern for the company. Of course, no one wanted to ask any questions after enduring twenty minutes of such a lousy presentation.

Unfortunately, some men approach some Bible classes in a similar fashion in that they are not genuinely interested in the subject they have been called upon to teach. Their attitude (week after week) must be endured by the participants because it is typically the only study for adults at that time. In this type of environment some will choose to miss the class rather than suffer through it. This happens more than Christians would like to admit.

The purpose of this chapter is to help us recognize that as teachers we have a huge impact on the attitude and level of participation from the class. It is important that this be understood so that, even if it is not the favorite topic of the teacher, it will still be taught as if it were, and this zeal must be genuine.

"Be enthusiastic about your subject. An instructor's enthusiasm is a crucial factor in student motivation. If you become bored or apathetic, students will too. Typically, an instructor's enthusiasm comes from confidence, excitement about the content, and genuine pleasure in teaching" (*Tools For Teaching,* 196). Confidence as a teacher comes from knowledge of the word of God. With good comprehension of the subject from Scripture, the teacher will feel adequately prepared to stand before adults and direct a study. This depth of study will naturally produce an excitement about the content of the class. It will then be a joy to share what you as the teacher have learned from your personal study. It is impossible truly to be enthusiastic about a subject you have not studied. We must be careful not to deceive ourselves as teachers.

Keeping A Pleasant Demeanor

Everyone has a day that goes badly. Everyone has a day when he does not feel well. Within the church you will find the most sympathetic and understanding group to stand before. However, that is no reason to demonstrate a poor attitude before the class. No matter what has happened earlier in the day, the task before you is to be a pleasant, enthusiastic teacher for the next forty-five minutes. Everyone is capable of putting his best foot forward when he wants to, and anyone teaching needs to see a need to maintain the same disposition from week to week.

Remember, we work very hard as teachers to create an environment within the class. Hopefully we are creating an environment of interest, discussion, learning, and edification. If the teacher's demeanor changes from week to week, even a little, the fragile environment of trust and engagement will quickly disintegrate and will be very difficult to recapture. What is needed is stability from the teacher.

The teacher must not run into class at the last minute. The participants gain confidence in the teacher by seeing him present well in advance of the start time. Additionally, have your notes set out, have your Bible open and be physically standing before the class a few minutes prior to the beginning of class. This will help everyone to settle and be ready to begin at the appointed time. I would advise a quick last glance at your notes to keep the main objectives in mind. Many in the class will mimic your behavior and actions. Imagine a class where everyone is in his seat ready to begin three to four minutes in advance, and everyone is looking at his Bible or notes!

At the appointed time the teacher needs to begin the class. Your first words will set the tone for the remainder of the class; therefore, make them pleasant words. Begin with a greeting, a warm welcome to visitors, politely asking people to open to the first passage, and looking at the appropriate class material. Smile a lot! This should not take more ten to thirty seconds. Keep it short, but be very courteous and pleasant.

Demeanor is evidenced in tone of voice, physical expressions, response to questions, and more. The easiest way to ensure a steady demeanor is to be yourself when standing before the class. Genuineness cannot be faked. Therefore, maintaining a godly character in life will aid greatly when teaching. When emotions are affecting us, we must work harder to divorce ourselves from those things that would distract us and settle into a more common, habitual demeanor. Variety as a teacher is a good, but not in the professional demeanor that is maintained before the class.

Body Language Speaks Volumes

There are many publications on the market about body language which you are encouraged to examine. My point here is merely to mention a few things which are common.

Ask anyone who stands before people on a regular basis, and you will quickly hear that posture is important. If you want to portray confidence, you must stand confidently. Square your shoulders, straighten up, stand tall. If you have prepared well for the class, this should not be too difficult. It will make a big difference about how you think of yourself, and will strongly impact how you are perceived.

Leaning on the lectern conveys that the teacher is tired. Before the class begins, before you even speak, the class is watching your body language. Convey confidence and enthusiasm for your task. In the last three minutes, when standing at the lectern, frequently look up and smile, perhaps with a small wave of recognition to someone who has just come in.

Crossed arms is one of the worst postures to use in front of a group. It conveys great negativity, as if you really do not want to be there or wish the person speaking would just be quiet. People who are angry and upset frequently cross their arms. Obviously when trying to establish and maintain an atmosphere of discussion, this is a posture the teacher should avoid.

Hands can be a problem for many. What do you do with them? Many novice teachers (including me) will at first hold on to the lectern as if it were a life preserver and they are drowning! Other folks tend to wring their hands, or pop their knuckles. If we are not careful, our hands can become a visual distraction to the extent people are not listening to what is being said. Therefore any of this sort of behavior must be avoided.

To put your hand in your pocket or not to put you hand in your pocket, that is a good question. Depending on who is asked, you will get different responses. If you choose to use your pocket while speaking, never play with change or keys as these also become a distraction for others. My advice is never to use your pocket while speaking, and only seldom use it when listening to others speak. Never put both hands into your pockets. That posture is as poor as crossing your arms and similarly conveys an attitude that says you would rather be somewhere else.

Expressions also convey our demeanor. When someone else is talking, it is important that we become a good listener! "Listen carefully to what students say. Be aware of the following:

- Content, logic, and substance
- Nuance and tone, including a speaker's degree of authority or doubt and degree of emotion or commitment
- How the comment relates to the overall discussion
- Opportunities for moving the discussion forward
- The mood of the class as a whole
- What is left unsaid" (*Tools For Teaching*, 69-70)

While listening it is important that the teacher convey his attention through eye contact, head nodding, an occasional "I agree," or something similar. While someone else has the floor it is rude continuously to glance at your watch, tie your shoe, or read your notes. Give attention to the speaker as this is the courteous attitude you expect from everyone else.

If you disagree with what someone else is saying that is not a good reason to change your demeanor. A poor attitude at that moment, a poor demeanor, or even a change in demeanor conveys a closed-mindedness that may or may not exist. Things to avoid would include: frowns, pained looks, vigorous negative head shakes, tapping fingers, or similar negative actions. Allow him to complete his statement, then answer in a way that is appropriate to your usual demeanor. I have found that this process will at times lead me to see my own error and I am compelled to give thanks for the person's courage to speak up.

The importance of eye contact cannot be emphasized enough. Physically turn your body to face the one making a comment, and look the person in the eye. Keep facing him until he has finished his thought, then turn back to the group. More importantly, keep your eyes off of your notes as much as possible. Try not to read to the class.

Look down as needed to get your thought, then just restate it as best you can from memory. Be careful to look at all of the group and not just the left side or the right side (as in a large auditorium class). You must visually include everyone in your comments by looking at them.

There is much that can be conveyed through a look. Salesmen understand the need to set a married couple shoulder to shoulder when trying to close the sale. Otherwise the "knowing looks" will pass between them and a silent decision will be reached while the salesman is talking. I can certainly remember, when I was a child, how much my upset father could convey in a glance. This being true, we must carefully and lovingly consider what is being conveyed with our eyes.

Furrowed brows, squints, raised eyebrows, painful looks—these are all non-verbal indicators which all adults are adept at reading. One of the best and easiest ways to understand what you are conveying as a teacher is to record yourself and review it at home. This is an exceedingly unpleasant experience, though it can be most useful in identifying problems. Anyone who teaches an adult class should try this at least once.

Overcoming Physical Distractions

Every person is unique, and most everyone has at least one annoying physical habit that distracts from his efforts at teaching the truth. I remember a young preacher I was helping who preached for me in private the third day we were together. In his twenty-five minute lesson I kept count how many times he said a certain word (well over 100 times) and when I told him about it, he did not realize it was happening. Other people may use the same hand gesture seventy-five times, or say a particularly favorite word in a peculiar way. Anyone who teaches or preaches has had to deal with such things.

Such physical or verbal distractions need to be overcome if the teacher truly wants to become effective. If left unchecked it will continue to distract, but may also become a point of disgust to the student. I can well imagine how the students may keep track of how many times the trait is observed and compare counts after class. I know I did that in at least one college class! To be effective, the teacher must be taken seriously. Language and behavior must be believable and appropriate.

There are a few techniques I have found useful in ridding myself of one of these poor habits. First, identify the problem and you will soon begin to "catch" yourself. After you observe yourself doing this once, be very sensitive not to allow it to happen again, understanding it will happen again. This process will begin to reduce the frequency of occurrence and eventually you will rid yourself of the troubling habit. If you are not catching yourself, enlist the aid of a spouse or friend. Ask them to keep a count and give it to you at the end of class. Be certain to thank them each time, especially as you are prepared to receive the bad news. This weekly "report card" will definitely cause you to begin catching yourself. Finally, record yourself several times. What we do not hear "live" we will usually hear on a recording. This could be audio only (which is helpful), but video would also enable you to see the physical distractions. Whatever is necessary, you must become aware of what you are doing in front of the group.

Secondly, write notes to yourself. Use an index card and a colored marker. Tape a note to yourself onto the lectern, perhaps like this: "Don't Pull Your Ear!" or "Don't Say *Great!*" If you are experiencing multiple problems, work on them one at a time until they become manageable.

Thirdly, charge yourself for a violation. Deny yourself some little thing (maybe a midnight ice-cream, or use of the T.V. remote) for a day. Find something that will help you get rid of the habit. This self-denial is healthy and will keep you focused on teaching the class during the intervening days.

Chapter 7
Preparing An Adult Class Curriculum

A yearly planning session to decide topics of study will aid the teacher in preparing materials in a less haphazard way. Bring your ideas to the elders in written form and reach an agreement (in advance) of what classes will be taught the following year. If you are at a congregation that does not have elders, a personal planning session will be equally helpful. I strongly recommend that planning occur. This will enable the teacher always to have a topic at hand to use in creating a workbook, or deciding on a workbook to purchase. There will always be a direction to take in our daily study efforts.

Master Schedule

A master schedule will be most useful in providing the teacher with an overview of all the classes being taught. This should include a curriculum of all the classes being taught, both children and adults. In large congregations there may be several adult classes taught concurrently. It is recommended that a one-page schedule be created in a quarterly grid. Simply divide a piece of paper into four equal parts (four quarters for the year). In each box label them Winter, Spring, Summer, and Fall. It is most helpful if all the class titles/topics are on one piece of paper.

This avenue makes it possible to plan a theme for the year's study in the adult Bible classes. When coupled with preaching on a topic for several weeks out of the year, a good emphasis can be placed on a needed area. Planning for a theme should involve the elders.

Their input will most likely identify where a specific need exists, and a theme phrase could be agreed upon before turning attention to specific classes. Topics can be developed and massaged months in advance, before they are presented to the congregation. Teachers can be arranged (if asked to write their own material), and given adequate time to prepare.

I would encourage some sort of "logo" approach to the theme (if being used). Place it on all materials produced that relate to that topic: Bible class workbooks, bulletin articles, sermon video presentations. I have frequently purchased business card magnets (available at your typical office store) which have a sticky back. Simply place your theme on a inkjet business card and print. It is quick, simple and very low cost. It enables the theme to have a place in the home of the believer where he will be reminded of it daily.

A good example of a theme might be: I Can Do More. The emphasis is obviously on growth, but the theme makes it personal. Suggested class themes which could profitably be studied in the realm of growth would include: Pressing On Toward Maturity In Christ; Paul's Attitudes About Growth; Becoming God's Instrument; and Training Our Senses.

Another good theme might be: Bringing In The Sheaves. Class topics might include: Biblical Approaches To Personal Work (examining the methods of Jesus, Paul, Peter and others); Important Teaching Passages (and how to use them); Utilizing And Creating Opportunities; and Personal Evangelism Nuts & Bolts.

The key to remember is that some of the classes should follow a theme for the year. It provides a unity to study throughout the year. A purpose and direction to study is always helpful in motivating people to study more on their own. Again, I emphasize that this process should be tailored to the needs of the congregation. Set these titles into a yearly grid being careful to arrange them in an order that seems appropriate. Other adult class studies can be added to complete the schedule as needed. Even if only one class focuses on the theme, this will help the congregation.

Collaboratively planning the class topics is both edifying and essential to a congregation. It speaks of care and attention to needs. I would not recommend following a theme every year as the uniqueness would be worn out. Planned subjects (even if not following a theme) should be determined at least yearly.

Weekly Schedule

About three months before materials need to be handed out for a class, the teacher needs to create a weekly schedule. Many aspects of this approach are discussed more fully in the chapter about Creating Original Materials. Using the topic assigned or selected, the teacher needs to decide what will be covered each week. This is more needed when teaching from materials created by someone else. The teacher needs to become *very* familiar with the material to have an idea of how long to spend on a subject in each class. If given a limited time (such as thirteen lessons), care must be given to divide the material into appropriate size portions. It is nearly impossible (for example) to teach a lesson on the character of Isaiah in one lesson. There is just too much material. Similarly it may be a stretch for some teachers to teach just one beatitude per lesson; there may not be enough information. If not given any time constraints, the teacher is still encouraged to plan carefully so as not to allow the class to be too long or too short. I can remember a class I sat in for two years on the book of Acts! The only truly memorable aspect of this class for me was that it was too long. Take care in creating this schedule. While it can be adjusted later, it is very helpful to create something useable.

After creating a one page overview, it is necessary to start writing something more specific for each lesson. I find a brief outline helpful, usually one lesson per page, or per half-page. Just a couple of thoughts to myself about the direction of the lesson. I will include and gather appropriate passages—all of the ones I plan to address. Basically I try to map out the lesson in my mind before I try to write it. By jotting it down like this, I can return to it within a few days and contemplate the lesson again and make any necessary modifications. By the time I actually begin to type the lesson, I am prepared with something to say that is meaningful, since I would have been thinking about the lesson for several days. I try to write one lesson a week, but I also write a weekly schedule before I start—basically an expanded overview of the class. It helps me stay focused on the direction of the class and keeps the individual lessons in the proper context.

Balanced Topic Selection

A good mix of textual studies and topical studies will keep the brethren interested in attending and preparing for classes. It is one way to generate enthusiasm and foster edification within the congregation. If your congregation's Bible class period has a huge difference in attendance numbers from your worship assembly, you might try changing what you as the teacher are doing to generate interest. Varying the type of study and the topics of study is effective.

For example: can you imagine a class that covers all four gospel accounts, one after another? I doubt that anyone would attempt such a class for many reasons. One reason would be that the subject matter is very repetitive. Sadly we are not always as careful of such things when moving from purchased workbook to workbook. The overall plan of study is much more haphazard, sporadic, even careless unless we make a point of planning the year's study. Variety in types of studies is very important and needs to weigh heavily in the decision process of classes to be taught, as well as the order of classes.

Curriculum is an important consideration that every educator recognizes. The choice of materials is crucial, as well as how the teacher plans to use them. For the Bible teacher these choices are more than crucial, they are essential. We are helping people to learn the will of God. Paul was careful to declare the whole counsel of God (Acts 20:27), and we must do the same. We must be careful to leave nothing out. The more we can plan and think about curriculum, the more successful and meaningful our Bible classes will become.

Chapter 8
Creating Original Materials

Within my lifetime the advent of desktop publishing has changed the entire concept of Bible class materials. No longer are we restricted to professionally published booklets. With effort and study, a good workbook can be produced on a computer and printed with a low end digital black and white copier. Most congregations can afford this and the resulting class will typically be more effective if the teacher is presenting his own material.

Purpose Of A Workbook

The novice teacher will most likely use a purchased workbook, so I will assume if you are reading this you have taught a few adult classes. The inexperienced teacher will use a workbook as a guide for their own study and it gives direction to the class. Most elders wisely insist that a book of some sort be used to provide order and stability to class studies.

I did not start preaching until I was 34. I sat in many adult classes before I started teaching them. One of the least effective classes and least memorable, are the ones where the teacher gives you a handout as you walk in the door. This will usually be one piece of paper with perhaps five or six questions on it. I understand that many of the people teaching adult classes have full time jobs in the world (as I have had), but to hand out materials just as class begins reflects little preparation on the part of the teacher.

As a student I seldom filled in the questions in such a class, because I did not want to miss any of the discussion or lecture from the teacher. After class that piece of paper ended up folded in half in the front of my Bible, along with other pieces of paper. After several weeks of dropping papers out of my Bible I would usually throw them all away and start over filling up the front of my Bible. If I tried to compile them all into a notebook I invariably lost a few and thus had an incomplete record of the study.

The main purpose of a workbook is to guide the student in study and preparation for the actual class period. From an educational standpoint, very little will be retained by the student if there has been no preparation prior to the discussion period. "If the class comes in and hasn't studied its lesson, the teacher isn't likely to get much meaningful discussion and participation" (*Success At Bible Teaching*, 114). Discussions will be richer, deeper, and more applicable if students have had an opportunity to look at the material, and more importantly, examine Scriptures that will impact the study. In addition, the student will complete the class and have all the lessons in one location with his notes to refer back to in the future. I have several workbooks from classes I participated in more than twenty years ago. When I look back through the booklets and my notes, it is amazing what can be recalled. Those books are valuable to me since they represent one avenue of growth for me as a Christian.

Therefore, I contend that a good workbook is of great benefit to the student, but also to the teacher. It is highly recommended that a complete workbook be handed out one week prior to the class beginning, giving the students one week to complete the first lesson. Most students will thumb through the book, or at least read the table of contents to gain an overview of the complete study. As the teacher and the student enter the first class, both will have a good grasp of what material or topic is being considered.

Deciding On A Topic

Getting started has got to be the most difficult part of creating a workbook. Unless a topic has been assigned to you, it is likely you will sit down with a Bible, a pad of paper and a pencil to begin brainstorming. Sometimes after a serious attempt I might write down several good ideas. Frequently I end up with one or none and I throw the paper away in disgust.

If teaching on a set passage of Scripture (like The Sermon on the Mount from Matthew 5-7), or on a specific book (like Hebrews), then your topic has been assigned, even if you assigned it to yourself. I typically try to teach two to three specific book studies a year (in either the Sunday or Wednesday adult Bible class). A greater scope of study involving all the classes taught over a four to six year period should include a complete study of the New Testament during that period of time (see the chapter on Curriculum). These workbooks may be less complex than a topical study, but should also be prepared in advance.

More frequent in my experience has been the need to create a topical study encompassing thirteen to twenty-six lessons. If the teacher has been given no direction, some important decisions will have to be made. Reducing options helps a teacher focus on a subject. Consideration must be given to classes previously taught and how long ago. It can be good to present some material again, even in the same format. Most Bible studies can be lumped into a few categories. Try thinking in these categories to see where you (as the teacher) desire to lead a study:

A book of the Bible
Character Study (one or more people)
Fundamentals of Faith
False Doctrines
Scheme Of Redemption/Biblical Themes
(like Love, or Commitment)
Evangelism
Christian Evidences
Create your own categories

Once a category has been decided, then work to narrow the field further. For example: a character study on Barnabas would be difficult for thirteen weeks, however if coupled with other preachers who traveled with Paul it may be possible to create an interesting study. Another example: a study of every false doctrine is not feasible in a thirteen or a twenty-six week study. So you must decide which false doctrines you desire to cover—the tenets of Calvinism (T.U.L.I.P.), and/or modern Pentecostalism, and/or others. In this fashion a strong series of topics can be organized in an effective way.

One Page Overview

Once a topic has been narrowed down to a decision, take one piece of paper and write down all thirteen or twenty-six lesson titles. It will be very helpful at this point if you will take the time carefully to consider each lesson and write down appropriate references you wish to include. Additionally I would recommend a few sub-headings for each lesson.

For example if creating a workbook on Evidences and lesson four is about archeological proofs that the Bible is accurate, it will be very helpful later to have listed 3 or 4 specific proofs you have in mind to examine. Gather those materials later, this is just an overview. Those specifics can always change later.

If writing a workbook on redemption language and lesson ten is about reconciliation, some good sub-headings might include: the gospel of reconciliation, Jesus breaking down the dividing wall and reconciling the differences between Jews and Gentiles, as well as a few thoughts about enmity.

If this process is followed for each and every lesson you are considering, you will end up with a very good outline to follow—all on one piece of paper. You can always reject a specific lesson if you decide it is not working as well as the others. For this reason I have written workbooks that are nine lessons, twelve lessons, fifteen lessons, twenty-one lessons, and more. Don't get stuck on thirteen or twenty-six lessons unless that time constraint has been placed upon you. You may also do well to consider if some of your planned lessons will take more than one class period to teach.

No one will ever see this piece of paper except you. Keep yourself organized at this point. You may end up with two or more pieces of paper with overviews of classes. This will help you decide which class topic is working better without having to devote serious amounts of time, finding out too late, and being stuck presenting material you really do not think is all that good. I have been there!

By using an Overview sheet on a regular basis you will end up with several unused class ideas which will help in creating a yearly scope of study. It will also enable you to keep a class idea alive in your mind on the back-burner so that when the time comes to begin writing, you are ready with something to say.

An overview is a means of organizing time and thoughts into avenues to utilize effectively what precious time you have to devote to such materials. It seems like you may be spending a lot of time doing this, especially the first time. In the long run you will have spent less time and end up with a more organized thought-through workbook.

Creating A Layout

Once a decision has been reached on the subject, and an overview sheet has been prepared, it is finally time to begin creating the workbook. Some consideration should be given to which computer program should be used, especially if you will be taking it to a professional printer. Microsoft Word can be difficult to work in, but I produce most of my workbooks with it. Microsoft Publisher can be easier. Ultimately, use the program you are most comfortable and proficient with. This will enable you to get the look you want.

What size paper will you use? A standard sheet in a portrait orientation is the easiest because it requires no folding or stapling. Generally this will utilize a comb or edge type binding. Pages will print just like normal with no special set up. If using a different size paper or orientation, be certain to think through the entire workbook giving consideration to margin sizes, gutter sizes, and how close your printer will print to the edge of the page.

Creating Original Materials

I recommend creating a document of about twenty pages before you begin working. On page one type "cover." On page two type "table of contents." Set page three on your screen so that you can see the entire page. It is now time to create a layout for each lesson that will be copied and pasted into all the lesson pages. You are not writing material at this point, but creating a layout. A good hour or two spent here will enable you to finish the project more quickly later on in the process.

The easiest layout is a simple text box that fills the entire page. I would recommend you create the following:

1. A text box with "Title" in it. Set the font and size now.

2. A larger text box with "Body" in it. Set the font and size now.

3. Create page numbers for the document.

With these created, try manipulating the background fills to create a multicolor effect—even with black, grey and white. A laser printer will do a remarkably nice job of the various shades on a blended fill. You can even add an additional empty box just to gain a color on the page, or to create a geometric effect with a shape or group of shapes.

A decision will need to be made if you plan to write an article for each lesson, merely ask questions, or a combination of both. This will affect the layout of your first page. I would encourage you to write an article, much like a bulletin article, though it does not have to be as long. Do not feel obligated to fill the entire page with text—try for an artsy appearance. Maybe use two-thirds of the page oriented toward the lower right corner. Use the rest of the page for a heading, lesson number, main text or reading, perhaps even the title of the workbook.

If creating an article, you will need to create a second page at this time which would be the back-side of the lesson. More pages can be added if you desire. On the second page most teachers would place questions. I would encourage you to create two or three separate text boxes on the page of uniform or different sizes in which you can place questions. Give some thought to how this page looks—where you have placed the boxes. Consider a tall narrow box with two wider boxes. Consider using a text box for quotations from Scripture, a scientific resource, or a book of false doctrine, that fits your topic. Place a word in each text box to represent what you intend to do with each box, for example: Questions, Applications, Quotes. Set your font and sizes now.

Will you be using any art? If you plan to include some art in each lesson, create a uniform text box to place it in so that it will be in the same location for each lesson sheet. For example: if a piece of art is used to associate with each lesson, you may desire to place this near your heading. If the workbook is about The Church you may desire to gather pictures of people worshipping. Use art sparingly and in a small size—not bigger than about one or two inches square. It should add to the project, not take it over or distract from it. If appropriate material cannot be found for every lesson, just leave it off a lesson now and then. When I wrote a workbook on Psalms I used artwork throughout of ancient scrolls. The artwork unified the lessons into a theme. Not every workbook needs art. Care should be taken not to violate copyright laws when using images from the internet. I prefer to use photos since they copy so well on a digital printer. They really enhance the workbook and give it a much more professional appearance.

Once your layout for the first lesson is complete, copy and paste it onto the following pages. You should end up with a full size workbook (appropriate number of pages and lessons) that is completely void of substance. Be sure to save your work!

Creating A Cover

To create a cover a decision must first be made about what type of cardstock or paper it will be printed on. I typically use a heavy cardstock (say 90 to 120 lbs). The color of the paper may affect color choices you make for fonts or photos. I print the covers in color on an inkjet printer. It really does not cost much and makes the workbook appear more professional.

Look for one piece of art that captures the flavor of your topic. For a workbook on "Christian Sacrifices" you might look for a great photo or public domain oil painting of an animal sacrifice. There is a lot of great art of this sort on the internet. Use it. Place the photo on the cover so that it fills about one-third to half the page. Create a text box for the title of the book. Set font and size. I would also encourage you to create another text box to include the location of the class, perhaps the teacher, the season and year, etc. Set font and size. This information should be substantially smaller than the title. Print a sample of your cover, and lesson one to examine in hard copy. Make any changes or adjustments you think are needed.

With the advancements in desktop publishing there is no reason for anyone to produce ugly class materials. Why hand out a piece of white paper with six questions, when it could be on a nicer piece of paper, with a piece of art, and three or four shades of tinting? If the teacher will take the time to make the page look good, I believe the teacher will then take the time to ask an appropriate number of quality questions.

Creating Content With Substance

Over the next several weeks you will be working to write the lessons. If you have done the work in creating a layout, all that is left is to fill in the boxes. You will know what your length needs to be based on the size of the box. If you find you need more room, reduce the font size. If you need less, increase the font size. The point is to fill the box. If you feel the box is the wrong size, change it—but change it on all the lessons so that there is a uniform appearance (if possible).

In writing an article about the lesson topic, be careful not to "give away" everything you want the students to discover in their study of Scripture. It may be helpful at this point to make a decision about which passages of Scripture will be covered in the questions, and which could be quoted in the article. The concept here is to create a simple article that touches on most of the aspects that you intend for the students to learn.

For example, if your lesson is about 1 Corinthians 1 it would be appropriate to include the following aspects in your article in a brief way: our need to listen to the apostle's writing; the continuance of problems in the church as a result of the attitudes of the world creeping in; provide a couple of modern issues facing believers in regard to division and following the thinking of men. There are still many specifics from the chapter that can be addressed in a series of questions, but the student has a good framework to structure his thoughts about this topic.

Reserve the substance of the lesson for the questions you will write. Allow the students to see in Scripture the points you are trying to make. Allow them to discover applications from the text, through your guided questions. In doing so, the class period will be made ripe for discussion. You as the teacher will not have told them everything in advance, but will have pointed them in the right direction.

Creating Effective Questions

Writing good questions is an art-form. Take some time in formulating your questions. Try writing the same question four or five different ways, then pick the best one. A question is a point of discovery for the student.

I fear a lot of times in the class materials we create we want to just tell them everything. There is no discovery. The concept of discovery in Bible study is one of the things that led me personally to begin searching the Scriptures more diligently—I was discovering truth. I was learning and seeing things for myself. We want to foster discovery through our questions.

A good lesson will incorporate several styles of questions. A poor lesson will ask all the same type. Consider the following list of question types that can be utilized effectively:

- Fill in the blank
- Multiple choice
- Tell me the facts
- Provide a Scripture to support or deny

Creating Original Materials 67

- What does the context indicate
- Complete the chart
- How do these other passages impact our understanding?
- Please explain . . .
- Compare and contrast
- What does the world say . . .
- Provide two applications
- Many more!

We have all sat in a class with a set of materials in front of us that was all fill in the blank, or all true/false. Variety in the type of questions will foster interest in further study and being prepared for the discussion period. At times it is beneficial to lump two or three types of questions into one group (such as applications or telling what the Scriptures teach).

Thought questions that require little thought are not good questions. Even the mature Christian should be challenged in some of the questions, usually in the realm of application. Some folks need to learn the facts. "There are times when it is appropriate to check student background knowledge with a series of brief factual questions" (*McKeachie's Teaching Tips,* 39-40). The job of the teacher is to balance these various levels of learning and help everyone. Therefore, each lesson should have some easier and harder questions.

As you are filling in the boxes on lesson one, be sure to consider carefully what questions you are asking. Many times the series of questions on an outline is leading the student to a point of discovery—most frequently in the application. After the questions are written, double-check the order of your questions to see if something needs to be moved.

How many questions should be included? I usually limit it to about ten, unless the material is on a passage of Scripture. I wrote eighteen questions on Ephesians 4. I also planned to study that material for about three weeks, and it took longer due to the great amount of discussion. Four to five questions is usually so few the student answers them very quickly or not at all, and twenty questions is so many they feel overwhelmed and pressured for time so that they are left blank. As a teacher, find a proper balance based on the maturity and study habits of the congregation. Tailor the materials to the needs of the congregation.

Leave appropriate spaces on the page for people to write down answers. This tells them you expect them to study and write something down—but you will not have to announce it.

At this point, let's consider a few sample "poor questions" which can be adapted into "better questions." The key is to keep in mind some of the concepts of allowing the student to discover truth.

Poor Question #1 – Blessed are the poor in spirit for they shall _____.

Better Question #1 – How will those who are poor in spirit be filled?

The poor example simply regurgitates an answer from the Bible. The better question forces the student to discover the meaning or at least try to understand it.

Poor Question #2 – Jesus said to "love your enemy." (True or False)

Better Question #2 – Using a Bible dictionary or *Strong's Concordance*, examine the Greek word *agape* which is translated "love" and explain how we are to love our enemy.

Again, the "better question" forces the student to travel a course of discovery. This question would not be a true challenge for those who had been a Christian for several years, but it is a good intermediate level question.

Poor Question #3 – List the seven points of unity in Ephesians 4:3-5 which begin with "one."

Better Question #3 – For each of the seven points of unity in Ephesians 4:3-5 which begin with "one," explain how there is actual unity or dissonance in religious thinking today.

This "better question" forces application of the text into modern discussion. This type of question will be much more effective in generating discussion.

> **Poor Question #4** – Which church in Asia was condemned for being "lukewarm"?
>
> **Better Question #4** – Give two other phrases which in your mind are equivalent to being "lukewarm." What trait is being condemned?

The point of discovery in this question is the idea of connecting modern phrases to biblical phrases. Comments and discussion in class should bring out concepts like "bench-warmer" or "back-rower." There are several other similar phrases all which point out a lack of commitment, a lack of true zeal.

As the teacher works at creating good, quality questions, the participants will desire to relate what they have discovered or what good thought they had. This allows class discussion to extend beyond the actual question. If you are writing questions, you are encouraged to vary the type of question used, and not shy away from a complex question. Ask the questions that lead the students in learning from Scripture and making application.

Editing

After you have written all the lessons, you need to proofread it. I find this works better if I work from a hard copy. I take a marker or red pencil and circle everything I see that needs to be corrected. After examining the entire document, go to the computer and make corrections.

When you think you have everything looking right, print it again. Take this to a friend and ask him to proofread it. My wife usually gets this job. Invariably the proofreader will find something you missed. That is good since it will make your project look more professional. Have the proofreader to verify that your art choices are appropriate and that they do not distract but in fact enhance the page.

Binding

Once all your pages have been copied, your covers have been printed, and everything has been collated, you still need to bind it. The worst thing you can do is smack a staple in the top corner. We all have materials bound in this way. The covers tear off and the pages get bent and creased. If all you have available is a stapler, then put three staples vertically down the left edge. You could dress it with some old fashioned colored binding tape (such as is still seen on book bindings at the public library). This is a much better binding, but still tends to look unprofessional.

I would encourage you to use a comb binding or clip binding or some other professional means of binding. Plan to spend about $1 a book on the cover paper and a binding. A good binding keeps the materials looking nice, even when people are carrying it back and forth sometimes for six months. Any print shop can tell you binding options, and most binding machines can be purchased relatively cheaply.

Remember, the main purpose of a workbook is to guide the student in study and preparation for the actual class period. It should not tell everything you know on a subject—save some for the class period. It should not be encyclopedic in that it is so long and so heavy people would be less likely to use it.

The best workbooks are the ones that get used. They become the memorable classes and the life-changing studies. That is an effective adult class.

Using Purchased Workbooks

Though less desirable, a purchased workbook can be an effective teaching tool in an adult Bible class. The main difficulty is when a writer includes a question that makes perfect sense to him, but has no apparent correct answer to anyone else. This is generally a poorly written question, which I will admit I have been guilty of.

At times the teacher is given the workbook at the same time it is handed out to the class. This is a worst case scenario. At the very least we would hope to have a copy of the book a couple of weeks before it is to begin. Two to three months would be more of an appropriate time for the teacher to take a good look at the book, examine the sequence of lessons and read through each question. If a question does not make sense to the teacher (who must teach it), then I suggest replacing it. Tell the class (a week before) that you are removing the question or give them a better question to lead them where you want the discussion to go.

Most workbooks on the market have an article followed by questions. The questions are generally answered in the article. Therefore during class it should not be necessary to go over what was written in the article. It would be appropriate perhaps to read a short quotation at times, but the material covered in the lesson should be presented by the teacher in his own vernacular. I recommend using very little "lecture" in a class setting—actually as little as possible. It is not the best learning style for a class environment.

Allow me a moment to say that preaching *is* appropriate and is the God-given means by which the word is to be proclaimed (Rom. 10:14; 1 Cor. 1:21). Even in a private setting, preaching and teaching are intermixed. However, the purpose of a public Bible study is to learn together. My training as a teacher tells me discussion is the best format for this environment. The teacher's job becomes one more closely associated to a moderator than a lecturer. This is an effective class (see Chapter 2).

When using a workbook written by someone else, great care should be taken to be certain the book is biblical. Do not be afraid to point out where you do not agree with the workbook. The workbook was written by a man, and the lessons are often unclear, misunderstood, or simply wrong. As long as we teach the Bible, any workbook can be an effective tool. I would not recommend using a workbook full of known errors or opinions.

Many workbooks still used in congregations today are written by men who are still living. It may be possible to contact the author if you have a question about a workbook question, or a point being made in an article. Do not be afraid to ask. Letters, e-mail, and phone calls can prove helpful in teaching someone else's material and the men who have written the booklets will most often be pleased to field your questions. They may even ask for feedback on how the material was useful.

Generally, someone else's workbook must be adapted for your own use. Consider the workbook a general guide for the study, but do not feel restricted to the topics, lessons, or questions contained in the workbook. Branch out extending the discussion or applications into areas perhaps not covered in the book.

I find that most purchased books do not have enough writing space for my notes. I recommend using another notebook for typed notes. As with *any* class, be certain that you as the teacher fully understand the topic and answers prior to beginning the class. If touching on a point that is "shaky" in your own understanding, that is when you should stick very close to your notes—even reading them to be certain you are not misunderstood. It takes effort, but using a workbook is a very effective means of teaching Bible classes.

Chapter 9
Practical Tips

Student Feelings

- If the student feels rushed, check your pace and allow for more comments.
- If the student feels unchallenged, check how well you are asking questions.
- If the student feels bored, check how much opportunity you provide for discussion.
- If the student feels lost in the discussion, check how frequently you refocus on the topic.
- If the student feels like no progress is being made, check how well you are staying on topic.
- If the student feels like missing the Bible Class, check your enthusiasm as the teacher.
- If the student feels unwelcome to make comments, check your expressions and tone.
- If the student feels dumb, check your demeanor.

Presenting

- Do not use the same gesture repeatedly.
- Use a conversational language and tone. Be yourself.
- When answering a question, speak to the entire class.
- Make good eye contact with individuals when speaking or listening.
- Use your notes as little as possible. Know your material.

- Notes can plagiarize! When said well, use it!
- Speak up, even when amplification is used.
- Limit the amount of lecture.
- Be a good listener!

Questions

- Pay attention to student answers.
- Ask a person if you have answered his question.
- Thank a person for asking a question, especially a hard question.
- When you ask a question, wait for the answer—even if it is a long wait.
- Restate questions, looking at the one who asked, to be certain you received it correctly.
- Without applications, the student will not remember the point of the context.
- Questions should be used to check for student understanding.

General

- Stay in the context.
- Expect more from the class!
- A consistent demeanor is a must!
- If something is not working well, try a different approach.
- Do not try everything at once. Only do what you are comfortable doing.
- Do not get stuck in a rut doing everything the same way every time the class meets.
- Restate comments or questions from others which might not have been heard well.

Methods & Techniques

- Hand out all the lessons one week before the study begins.
- Have notes out and be standing before the class a few minutes early.
- Students also need to prepare mentally for a study. There is a real need for brief review.

Practical Tips

- Do not allow the class to become bogged down in the review.
- Defer answering questions to another person in the class.
- If asked a hard question, ask the same thing of the one who questioned you.
- Have extra application questions prepared in advance and written down.
- If you convey an expectation, there also needs to be an explanation as to why you expect the student to do this.

References

Brinkley, Sam Jr. and Martin M. Broadwell. *Success At Bible Teaching.* Athens (GA): Publishing Systems, Inc., 1973.

Davis, Barbara Gross. *Tools For Teaching.* Hoboken (NJ): John Wiley & Sons, Inc, 2001.

Malouf, Doug. *How To Teach Adults In A Fun and Exciting Way.* Crows Nest, Australia: Allen & Unwin, 2003. Http://www.allenandunwin.com.au.

McKeachie & Svinicki. *McKeachie's Teaching Tips* (12th Edition). Boston: Houghton Mifflin Company, 2006.

McKenzie & Harton, *The Religious Education Of Adults.* Macon (GA): Smyth & Helwys, 2002.

Meyer, Leo. *Teach! The Art Of Teaching Adults.* Hayward (CA): LAMA Books, 2005.

www.ingramcontent.com/pod-product-compliance
Lightning Source LLC
Chambersburg PA
CBHW031418040426
42444CB00005B/619